60

JAN   2001

cool collectibles
COINS

Jennifer Abeyta

HIGH interest books

Children's Press
A Division of Grolier Publishing
New York / London / Hong Kong / Sydney
Danbury, Connecticut

For my grandparents, Raymond and Florence Beyer,
for beginning our family tradition in coin collecting

Book Design: Lisa Quattlebaum
Contributing Editor: Mark Beyer

Photo Credits: p. 5 © Daemmrich/The Image Works; p. 6 © Archive Photos/
Lambert; pp. 8, 18, 20, 25, 31 by Laz Burke; p. 11 © R. Lord/The Image Works; p. 14
© Corbis/Bettmann; pp. 22, 37 © Corbis/Bettmann-UPI; p. 32 © Super Stock; pp. 35,
39 © American Numismatic Association.

Visit Children's Press on the Internet at:
http://publishing.grolier.com

Library of Congress Cataloging-in-Publication Data

Abeyta, Jennifer.
   Coins / by Jennifer Abeyta.
      p. cm.—(Cool collectibles)
   Includes bibliographical references and index.
   Summary: Surveys the history of coin minting in the United States, explains what
factors determine the value of collectible coins, and offers ways to start a collection.
   ISBN 0-516-23329-7 (lib.bdg.) ISBN 0-516-23529-X (pbk.)
      1. Coins, American—Collectors and collecting–Juvenile literature. [1.
Coins—Collectors and collecting.] I. Title. II. Series.

CJ1832 .A44 2000
737.4973'075—dc21

                                                    99-058254

CONTENTS

Introduction

People collect coins in different ways and for different reasons. Some people may like searching through their pocket change. Others may start a family collection and choose one day a week to look through coins together. Your parents or grandparents may have a cigar box filled with old coins. You may have already seen the new state quarters that can now be ordered from the United States Mint. These people are all coin collectors. They are numismatics. A numismatist collects coins, tokens, paper money, and even medals.

The first step in beginning any new interest is to learn about the subject. There is a difference between coin collecting and investing. Collectors are interested in the history, art, and design of coins. They buy coins to keep them,

Coin collectors often trade coins with other collectors.

not to make money from them. Investors buy
coins to make a profit. As soon as you learn
about coin collecting, you will begin to learn
which coins you will want to collect.

1

What Makes Coins Collectible?

MINT PRODUCTION

You probably know that coins are made at places called mints. The minting process is very important to coin collecting. Mint marks and minting errors are two things that make coins valuable.

Coins made for everyday use by people are called business strikes. Coins start out as blanks. These blanks are called planchets. They are metal circles cut out by a machine called a blanking press. The leftover metal is called webbing. Webbing is recycled. The penny (one-cent piece) is made differently from the silver-colored coins. The U.S. Mint sells copper and zinc to the coin makers. The coin makers then sell to the mint the blanks they cut.

The blanks are heated in a furnace to make them soft. They are then sent into the washer and dryer. The blanks are put into a machine that sorts usable blanks from bad blanks. This machine is called a riddler. Bad blanks are the wrong size or shape. The blanks that are used then go through an upsetting mill. This mill raises a rim around their edges. Now the striking process begins. Here the blanks are stamped with the designs and writing that make them real United States coins. A press operator inspects the new coins using a magnifying glass. The inspector looks for errors that may have happened

during the striking process. One such defect includes off-center strikes. Another defect is a light strikes. When this happens, the design is not deep or clear enough. There are also uneven strikes. Uneven strikes make the design too deep in one spot, but not deep enough in another. The coins then move through a sizer to get rid of the dented and bad ones. A machine counts the coins, and they are stored in bags. These bags are sewn shut and locked in vaults. The coins are then taken in armored trucks to the Federal Reserve Bank. Finally, the coins come to your local bank.

MINT MARKS AND ERRORS

The first letter of the city in which the mint is located is struck on coins as they are made. This is called a mint mark. The Philadelphia Mint started making coins in 1793. It still makes coins today. However, from 1793 to 1941, the Philadelphia Mint did not strike a mint mark on its coins. Collectors call these coins "plain." If you look through your pocket change, you might find a few pennies that don't have a mint mark. This is because the Lincoln penny is the only coin that the Philadelphia Mint still does not mark. The following chart shows where and when mints existed. It shows the letter you will find struck on each mint's coins. Also, the chart tells you if the coin is rare because of where it was struck.

City/State	Mint Mark	Years in Operation	Coin Rarity
Philadelphia, PA	P	1793–present	Errors only
San Francisco, CA	S	1854–1956; 1967–present	Errors only
Denver, CO	D	1906–present	Errors only
Charlotte, NC	C	1838–1861	All coins minted
Dahlonega, GA	D	1838–1861	All coins minted
New Orleans, LA	O	1838–1909	Errors only
West Point, NY	W	1984–present	Errors only
Carson City, NV	CC	1870–1893	Errors only

You should always check your pocket change for valuable coins.

Errors made during the minting process can be a collector's dream! Errors are coins that were not made right. Off-center coins are one type of error. This happens when part of the design is missing from the planchet. Another error is a coin struck on the wrong planchet. This happens when a nickel design is struck on a quarter blank. Also, coins without raised rims are errors. Coins that show multiple strikes are popular collectors' coins. Here, the blanks have been struck more than once. This leaves several partial impressions. Some blanks have left the mint without having been struck at all. There are also blanks that are missing metal or parts of the coin that are curved. From 1942 to 1945, nickel was not used in the five-cent coin. Instead, silver was added. Some of these blanks still exist and are rare and very valuable. Errors like this don't happen often, and no one knows exactly why they happen. Maybe a container of nickel blanks was sent to the quarter striker.

Maybe the striking press was feeding the blanks off-center. Who knows? Press operators can't possibly inspect every one of the millions of coins minted each year. Whatever the reason, numismatists gain from such mistakes.

CANADIAN COINS

The Royal Canadian Mint's Millennium Coins are an easy way for young collectors to start a Canadian coin collection. These coins are being introduced to commemorate the new millennium. Each month throughout 1999 and 2000, the Royal Canadian Mint will issue a new twenty-five cent coin.

The first series of coins celebrate the history of Canada. The second series will represent the goals for Canada's future. The twenty-four designs were chosen from over thirty-thousand entries to the Royal Canadian Mint's "Create a Centsation!" contest.

13

2

The History of U.S. Coins

COLONIAL AND AMERICAN COINS

The Massachusetts Pine Tree coin is a famous and beautiful coin. It was minted in 1652. It is not very rare and doesn't cost much. The Pine Tree coin is a coin that beginner collectors can easily find. However, many other colonial coins are very rare and cost a lot of money.

Benjamin Franklin and Paul Revere were two men who helped form the United States. They also helped to start American coin minting during Colonial times in the 18th century. Colonists used coins to buy things. After the Colonial period (1776), coin designs were made

Massachusetts Pine tree coins (shown front and back) date from 1652, but are not hard to find today.

for the newly formed nation. George Washington helped convince the federal government to make coins. He donated $100 to buy the silver to make enough coins to get started. Two thousand half-dimes were made from that silver. The Constitution finally gave the right of making American coins to the federal government in 1792.

Coins are divided into types. A coin type is one with a special design. Some of the many types, from Colonial to present times, are shown in the following chart. How many of these have you seen or heard of?

Cents	Half, Large, Flying Eagle, Indian, Lincoln
Nickels	Two Cent, Three Cent (Trime), Half, Indian Head (Buffalo), Shield, Liberty Head, Jefferson
Dimes	Bust, Seated, Winged Liberty Head, Roosevelt, Twenty Cents
Quarters	Bust, Seated, Liberty Head (Barber), Standing Liberty, Washington, 50 State
Half Dollars	Bust, Liberty Head (Barber), Walking Liberty, Franklin, Kennedy
Dollars	Bust, Peace, Morgan, Eisenhower, Anthony, Trade, Gold, Quarter Eagles, Three, Half Eagles, Eagles, Double Eagles, American Eagle Gold Bullion, American Eagle Silver Bullion

When important events happen, people want to remember them. Minting coins that show a scene from that event is one way to remember it. These coins are called commemorative coins. They are often created by famous artists. They always have beautiful designs. Most coin collectors interested in commemorative coins want a certain type. They want commemoratives made of silver between 1892 and 1954. These coins were not minted for circulation. A good example of a commemorative coin is the quarter that was minted for the World's Colombian Exposition in 1892. Another famous commemorative was the Pan-Pacific Exposition set (a set includes each of the different coins minted for that year). This set was minted in 1915 to raise money for that exposition. It was the most expensive set made until the Olympics sets began being made in 1983. Some modern-day commemoratives include the Statue of Liberty, Tribute to American Prisoners of War, and the Vietnam War Memorial. Others include the Constitutional Bicentennial (1976), and each Olympic Games.

THE NEW 50 STATE QUARTERS PROGRAM

The newest coins to be minted in America are the 50 State Quarters. Each quarter honors an American state. The quarters will be issued in the order in which each state became a member of the United States. The original thirteen states are being issued in the order that they signed the Constitution or joined the Colonial Union. Five new state quarters will be made each year for ten years, from 1999 to 2008. The chart

A new 50 State Quarter representing Georgia. Stamped on its back is Georgia's state symbol, the peach.

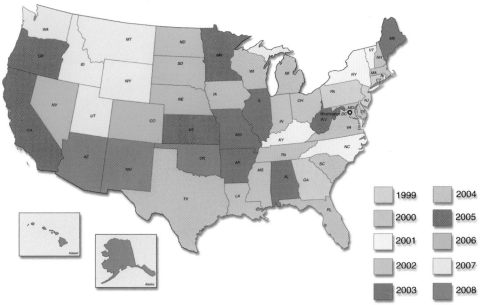

Each color shows the year that a U.S. state's honorary quarter will be issued.

above shows the fifty states quarters and the years in which they will issue.

These State Quarters show our nation's heritage. The "heads" side of the coin is a profile of George Washington. The "tails" side has a picture specially designed for each state. For example, the Delaware quarter shows Caesar Rodney riding a horse. Pennsylvania has the

The "heads" side of each 50 state quarter is the same. The "tails" side shows a special design for each state.

Commonwealth Statue. The New Jersey quarter has on it Washington's famous Delaware River crossing. Georgia's design is its famous peach. The Charter Oak is on the Connecticut quarter. Because the uncirculated coin set has not been used, these sets are considered to be in "mint condition." You can read more about conditions in Chapter Three.

You probably buy things almost every day. When you buy things, you often get change back. Don't be surprised to find this year's state quarters in your hand. You can start your own collection by saving and storing each state quarter from both the Denver and Philadelphia Mints. You can also buy an official U.S. Mint 50 State Quarters collector's map that has push-fit quarter holders (slots made to fit quarters). These holders make it easy for you to put in and take out your quarters. Each state has its own holder. Included with this map is some history about each state, the fifty state quarters, and the U.S. Mint.

The 50 State Quarters set and map don't cost much money. It's important to know that only a certain amount of uncirculated coin sets will be made. These are called limited editions. Only 1.5 million limited edition sets will be made. The Mint allows each household to buy only three sets. A State Quarters set would be a great gift for someone special.

The Value of Coins

CONDITION AND GRADING

Coin value is determined by its grade (how well it has been preserved). Coins that are uncirculated are considered to be in "Mint State." These coins hold Mint State (MS) numbers from 60 to 70. A grade of MS-70 is rarely given to a coin. This is because the moment the coin has been minted it begins to wear. Coins graded as Mint State have never been circulated or even touched by humans. Nor do these coins have any signs of wear on the high spots. High spots are the raised designs on the heads and tails sides of the coins. Circulated coins

Rare coins are often found in sunken ships. However, such coins usually go to museums so that everyone can admire their beauty.

Coins

are graded 1 to 59. The most common numbers and grades are Good (G), Very Good (VG), Fine (F), Very Fine (VF), Extremely Fine (EF), and About Uncirculated (AU). Proof sets are graded with a "P."

If you don't know what to look for, you won't be able to grade coins. Therefore, you must have a private grading service look at your mint coins. Here, coins are tested by several graders. If most agree upon a grade, it is given to the coin. After a certified service company grades your coins, it will place the coin in a hard plastic holder for its protection. There are three grading services that are respected in the business. These are the Numismatic Guaranty Corporation of America (NGC) located in Parsippany, New Jersey, PCGS Proof Coin Grading Service in Newport Beach, California, and ANACS in Columbus, Ohio.

The two types of grading are Mint State and Proofs. MS-65 is used to compare higher and

Collectible coins should be stored in air-tight containers for protection. Touching coins harms their grade.

lower grades. It is the average mint grade a coin can get. Higher grades are considered "super-grade" coins. MS–60 coins barely count as mint coins. Grades are also broken down by M–63 and M–67. These are reference points when a coin doesn't quite fit into other types. M–69 is about the highest grade you will ever see.

The grading of mint coins has a five-step process. The process looks at a coin's surface, luster, toning, strike, and eye appeal.

Surfaces

The more scratches on the coin, the lower the grade. Touching a Mint Condition coin could lower the grade. This will lower the value. It is important to hold a coin only on its outer edges. This way you will avoid harming its grade.

Luster

How a coin reflects light. A mirror-like reflection is best. A flat and dull reflection is the worst.

Toning

Toning is coloring. The slow process of toning creates a protective patina (darkening of color). Toning appears when coins are stored in a dry place. A silver coin will sometimes form on its surface colors of rose, blue, or gold. Experts are able to tell if a coin has been toned using a fake method. Toning is different from tarnishing. Tarnishing happens when a coin's surface

Proof set coins have never been touched by human hands.

becomes dull and spotted over a short period of time.

Strike
Strike is graded on the amount of detail and the sharpness of the strike.

Eye Appeal
If the coin has beautiful toning and few scratches or dents, it could be graded as appealing. This means it looks good. If a coin is totally tarnished and has scratches and nicks, it probably will be graded unappealing. This means it's ugly.

WHERE TO BUY AND SELL
There are people who buy, sell, and trade coins. They are called dealers. Sometimes dealers charge a lot of money for coins. These same coins can be bought through private collectors at a cheaper price.

Famous Collectors and Collections

Jerry Buss, who owns the Los Angeles Lakers, is well-known in the field of numismatics for his great collections that he keeps just for fun.

LaVere Redfield of Reno, Nevada, had over 400,000 silver dollars! A-Mark Corporation has since purchased this set for $7.3 million.

B. Max Mehl became a famous numismatist in 1928 when he advertised for sale "1913 Liberty nickels" for $50. He had 128,000 mail-order requests and made 30,000 shipments.

Mail order is a popular way to buy and sell coins. Certified Coin Exchange (CCE) publishes a newsletter with coin prices. Several magazines, such as Coin World, Coins, or COINage list coin prices for buying or selling. Coin dealers advertise in these magazines.

You can also find a list of auctions from magazines and the Internet. The Internet has many sites from which you can buy and sell coins. Some of the respectable companies and Internet addresses are listed under the Resources section at the end of this book. The U.S. Mint sells coins, too. Some coin sets can be bought from your local coin or collectibles shop. Check your hometown or city telephone book.

Popular magazines can keep you up-to-date on the latest trends in the exciting world of coin collecting.

Coins

PENNSYLVANIA ERROR QUARTER FOUND

DECEMBER

Mint Goofs

Error State quarter worth big bucks

Checking your coin for mint blunders

Bronze 1943 worth thousa

Holiday gift ide

If you colle

COINage

DECEMBER

HERE COMES THE NEW DOLLAR COIN

WILL IT WORK THIS TIME?

GOLD

COMES ALIVE

The Market Heats Up In Bullion And Rarities

Quarter Craze

The New Collectibles

Late U.S. Coin Prices

07 EX-HR
LET EDGE
$20
PR67
NORWEB

$3.99

4

Starting Your Own Collection

WHERE TO BEGIN

Hundreds of coins used every day have errors.
You can find such coins in your pocket change.
For instance, some of the 1982 Roosevelt dimes
don't have mint marks. The 1989 Washington
quarters don't have mint marks, either. Both are
supposed to have these mint marks. Why don't
they have the mint marks? Who knows? But the
fact that they don't is good for collectors. Very
few collectors have put together date and mint
collections of Roosevelt dimes or Washington
quarters from 1965 to the present. Building sets
of specific types of coins by date and mint mark

A magnifying glass can highlight any defects in a coin.

is a great way to start collecting. Trying to find and collect any of these series would be a fun family project or personal hobby. You can buy plastic holders called "two-by-twos" to store your coins. You can also buy coin albums.

The one-cent piece (what we call the penny), is a great place to start collecting. Pennies don't cost much money. There are many different types of collectible pennies worth hunting for. Some can be found in circulation. Most will be found at coin shows or through dealers.

Try looking for the Indian Head one-cent coins made of copper and nickel. These pennies were minted from 1859 to 1909. Indian Heads were replaced by the Lincoln cent (wheat pennies) in 1909. The tails of wheat pennies have a sprig of wheat on each side. The Lincoln Memorial-backed penny we use today replaced the wheat pennies in 1959. The Indian head or buffalo nickels were made before the Jefferson nickel.

There are many stories of people finding

Indian Head one-cent coins are easy to collect. They are not rare, and they don't cost much money.

valuable coins by looking them up in coin books. Galleries such as Heritage in Dallas, Texas, have coin books for people to look through. In California, one man bought an old silver dollar from a friend for one dollar. Neither of them knew it was worth $30,000! This is the price the buyer got from an auction! Another man inherited a cigar box filled with old proof sets of coins. He asked a Boston coin firm to look at the proof sets. The man received almost half a million dollars for them. Often, coin collecting magazines give examples of rare and valuable coins found in pocket change.

You can buy uncirculated proof coins from the U.S. Mint. Proof coins are struck two times or more on specially made blanks to give greater detail to the design. Proof coins are sold from the Mint during the year of issue for about ten times the value of each coin type. Proof coins are sold separately or in a set of denominations. Commemorative coins, such as the Olympics or Bicentennials and the new 50 State Quarters, are made in the same way as the proof coins. These are also sold in sets or separately.

With that in mind, the new 50 State Quarters are a perfect way to begin your collection. You are in the era of the 50 State Quarters! Any time is a good time to start collecting coins.

Commemorative coins, such as these coins that celebrate the Olympics, are easy to find and look great.

CARING FOR YOUR COINS

Do you like cleaning your room? Most of us don't. Maybe you don't like to do much cleaning at all. If so, coin collecting is the hobby for you. You don't EVER have to clean your coins. In fact, cleaning coins will harm them. Clean them

37

and they will be labeled as having been "cleaned" or "dipped." Also, fingerprints on coins can cause damage when stored over long periods. A coin dealer can sometimes clean your coin using a special chemical. However, cleaning coins should be done professionally.

Storing your coin collection is very important to guard its condition and grading. Collectors over the years have used envelopes, plastic holders, and wood cabinets. They've also used albums to store their coins. All of these are still used. However, you should be careful. Some of these supplies can damage the coins. Regular envelopes have chemicals in them that can rub off onto the coins. These chemicals will damage the coins. Some graded (grade is discussed in Chapter Three) coins are sealed in slabs (plastic holders). This type of storage has been used for less than ten years, so it is not known if the coins will suffer damage in later years. Some commemorative sets have been sold in "original copper frames." This

US
1 Dollar
1999

Two types of holders that keep your coins protected are the two-by-two (top and left) and the plastic "slab."

might tell you that the sets were issued in those frames. This is not true, but they do look nice.

The best way to store coins is in an airtight container in a cool, dry place. This way you will be able to enjoy looking at your coins and showing them to friends and family.

New Words

blanks   pieces of specially prepared metal used for coins

business strike a coin produced for circulation

bust   a person's portrait, usually from the shoulders up, which appears on the "heads" side of the coin

circulate to pass from person to person

commemorative a specially designed coin to honor a person, place, or event in history

condition   the physical appearance of a coin

denomination   the type and value of a coin, such as a penny, nickel, dime, quarter, half-dollar or dollar

design the portrait or picture on a coin struck on either side of the coin

die the metal with the design to be struck on a coin

edge   the thin round circumference of the coin, not the obverse or reverse

error   an improperly manufactured coin

grade the assigned condition of a coin determined by wear, luster, toning, strike, and eye appeal

luster the way a coin reflects light and the dull to shiny appearance of a coin

medal a circular piece of metal resembling a coin, given as an award

monetary having to do with money

mint a place that produces coins

mint mark the letter found on a coin representing the mint at which it was produced

mint set a full set of coin denominations from a particular mint

mint state the condition of a coin without wear, scratches, or dents

numismatics the collecting of coins, medals, and such of monetary value

numismatist a collector of coins

obverse the "heads" side of the coin with the design or portrait, mint mark, and date

off-center the design of a coin that is struck uncentered leaving a portion of the design omitted or not centered

patina a color that forms naturally on metals after a long period of time

plains coins that do not bear a mint mark

planchet a piece of metal or a blank on which a die is to be struck

proof a coin that is struck two times or more on a specially prepared, polished metal

proof set an uncirculated full set of denominations manufactured in a particular year

reverse the "tails" side of the coin

rim the raised portion of the edge of a coin

series all the dates and mint marks of a design in each denomination

strike the process of pressing or stamping a design onto a blank coin

toning the coloring a coin develops over time from the environment or chemicals

two-by-twos preservation containers made of plastic to house one coin

type the design of a coin

uncirculated a coin that hasn't exchanged hands, thereby showing no marks of wear, friction or fingerprints

For Further Reading

Books

Favis, Bill, and J.T. Stanton. *The Cherrypicker's Guide to Rare Die Varieties*, 3rd ed. Woleboro, NH: Bowers and Merena Galleries, 1994.

Russell, Margo. *Start Collecting Coins*. Philadelphia: Running Press Book Publishers, 1996.

Schwan, Fred. *Collecting Coins: Instant Expert*. Brooklyn, NY: Alliance Publishing, Incorporated, 1996.

Travers, Scott A. *One-Minute Coin Expert*, 3rd ed. New York: Ballantine, 1998.

Magazines

COINage. *Miller Magazines*, 2660 E. Main St., Ventura, CA 93003.

Coin Connoiseur. Coin Connoiseur, 5855 Topanga Canyon Blvd., Suite 330, Woodland Hills, CA 91367.

Coin World. *Ann Maria Aldredge*, Box 150, Sidney, OH 45365.

Numismatic *News and Coins*. Krause Publications, 700 E. State Street, Iola, WI 54990.

World Coin News. Krause Publications, 700 E. State Street, Iola, WI 54990.

Organizations

American Numismatic Association

Attn: Lawrence J. Gentile, Sr.

542 Webster Avenue

New Rochelle, NY 10801

(914) 632-5259.

(800) 367-9723

www.money.org

Professional Numismatists Guild, Inc.

Box 430

Van Nuys, CA 91408

http://web.coin-universe.com/png/

United States Mint

P.O. Box 382602

Pittsburgh, PA 15250-8602

www.usmint.gov

Web Sites

CoinMasters On-line Coin Club

http://www.coinmasters.org/mainpage.html

This site is dedicated to the coin trade education of its members. The club encourages learning the ethical standards of the hobby, along with active participation in coin collecting clubs. There are links to auctions and information for younger collectors.

Professional Coin Grading Service

http://www.pcgs.com

Here you'll find historical information on coin collecting and famous coins. You can also research articles on coin trading.

Index

About the Author

Jennifer Abeyta lives with her husband and three children in Oceanside, California. In addition to collecting 19th century coins, the Abeyta family is eagerly collecting the 50 State Quarters of the 20th and 21st centuries.